Wisdom for Victory

Eva Tano-Yeboah

Jesus Joy Publishing

First Published and printed in Great Britain in 2019 by Jesus Joy Publishing.

©Eva Tano-Yeboah, 2019

All rights reserved. The author gives permission for brief extracts from this book to be used in other publications provided that the following citation is stated: *'Wisdom for Victory by Eva Tano-Yeboah, 2019; Jesus Joy Publishing used by permission'*.

Scripture Quotations

Unless otherwise noted scriptures are taken from THE HOLY BIBLE, NEW INTERNATIONAL VERSION®, NIV® Copyright © 1973, 1978, 1984, 2011 by Biblica, Inc.™ Used by permission. All rights reserved worldwide.

Scriptures noted TMB are taken from The Message Bible New Testament. Copyright by Eugene H Peterson 1993, 1994, 1995. Used by permission of NavPress Publishing Group

Scriptures noted BSB are taken from The Holy Bible, Berean Study Bible, Copyright 2016, 2018 by Bible Hub Used by permission. All Rights Reserved Worldwide.

Cover Design

Cover design by Sabina Baaba Berko

ISBN 978-1-90797-163-1

Jesus Joy Publishing

a division of Eklegein Ltd

www.jesusjoypublishing.co.uk

04122019

Dedication

I dedicate this devotional to the Holy Spirit who in His power and gentleness directs us and transforms us - not giving up, 'till we become like Him.

Day 1

Take Cover

"God is our refuge and strength, an ever-present help in trouble. Therefore we will not fear, though the earth give way and the mountains fall into the heart of the sea."

Psalms 46:1

There are times in our lives when we have to deal with some challenging situations. They may be parenting issues, a friend going through a terrible time, problems in the family or a sickness here or there. Sometimes, it may seem like the world is crashing down on you and everything is falling out of place at the same time.

Your peace is challenged and your faith is tested. Have you ever been in a place where you were struggling to keep your cool?

Unanswered prayers, chaos, questions and the like may leave you feeling as if you have to deal with these things coming from different directions. One of you just isn't enough!

In times like these, God is your refuge and strength. Praise God!

We have a refuge prepared for us. God is our refuge and strength. If we run and take cover in Him, we will be safe. I encourage you to take cover in God, He is your strength. This verse goes on to state, *"therefore we will not fear, though the earth give way and the mountains fall into the heart of the sea."*

When you can't just keep up and the mountains seem to be shaking, your strength will come from hiding in the Lord. Spend time studying the Word, spend time praying honestly and talking to your Father. Get away from everything and take strength from your source. Go through today taking cover dear friend, knowing that He is our sure refuge and strength!

Take cover!

Strategy

> Surrender every situation completely to God (whether good or bad) and ask the Holy Spirit to give you grace to leave every care in His hands.

> Spend time praying and renewing your strength in the Lord. Spend time listening out for the voice and direction of the Holy Spirit.

Further reading

> Psalm 46

Day 2

Put Things in Perspective

"When Esau heard his father's words, he burst out with a loud and bitter cry and said to his father, 'Bless me - me too, my father!'"

Genesis 27:34

Jacob stole Esau's blessing. That was how I interpreted the passage above for quite a long time. Until I read the last two verses of the previous chapter:

"When Esau was forty years old, he married Judith daughter of Beeri the Hittite, and also Basemath daughter of Elon the Hittite. They were a source of grief to Isaac and Rebekah."

Genesis 26:34-35

Now let's put things in perspective. Esau lost the blessing of the firstborn because he married the daughters of the land in which they lived. His parents did not like it because those women did not worship God. As a result, Esau was a grief to his parents. Abraham took a wife for Isaac, but Esau did not allow Isaac to take a wife for him. He went ahead and married the women of the land who were not worshippers of the Most High God. Hence, God in His wisdom preserved the blessing by passing it to Jacob who in subsequent chapters married into the family of Rebekah.

The next time you think God has been unjust, put things in perspective. There is always a reason for a lost blessing, a missed opportunity or a delayed progress. Today, put things in perspective.

> "God is not human, that He should lie, not a human being, that He should change His mind. Does He speak and then not act? Does He promise and not fulfil?"
>
> *(Numbers 23:19)*

Strategy

Are there any consequences you're facing right now as a result of a careless decision? Have you lost an opportunity due to deliberate or non-deliberate disobedience? Ask the Lord to cover every mistake with the blood of Jesus and restore you back to His will.

Further reading

Genesis 27

Day 3

The Comforter

"... I will ask the Father, and He will give you another advocate to help you and be with you forever"

John 14:16

When Jesus was about to go to the cross He began to prepare His disciples for His departure. He started telling them some truths they were not ready for. They did not even understand them until His resurrection. One such truth was that He would pray the Father to give them *"another advocate"*. In other translations the same word is comforter.

When Jesus was on earth, He was a comforter and an advocate to His disciples. He empowered them, He gave them a sense of security and identity. The word *another* means a replacement for the same purpose. The Holy Spirit was a replacement of Christ in person for the disciples. And, just as He was for them then, He is for you and me today.

The Holy Spirit is the third member of the Trinity and He is with us forever! He will not leave you. He will be with you until Christ returns again. That is His role, to fill in the gap until Christ returns.

Do you feel alone? The Holy Spirit is with you. Do you need comfort or reassurance? The Holy Spirit is your comforter. Do you need counsel? He is your counsellor. Talk to Him, have fellowship with him, call on Him.

> "May the grace of the Lord Jesus Christ, and the love of God, and the fellowship of the Holy Spirit be with you all. Amen."
>
> 2 Corinthians 13:14

Strategy

Reflect on how you relate with the Holy Spirit. Is He an active part of your life or have you given Him a backseat? Pray and renew or strengthen your relationship with the Holy Spirit. Pray and submit yourself to the leading of the Holy Spirit.

Further reading

John 14

Day 4

The Company of Women

"... some women who had been cured of evil spirits and diseases: Mary (called Magdalene) from whom seven demons had come out; Joanna the wife of Chuza, the manager of Herod's household; Susanna; and many others. These women were helping to support them out of their own means."

Luke 8:2

Every narrative in the Bible is purposefully inscribed. This account of Luke concerning the women in the ministry of Jesus is not an accident. We get a snapshot of the people supporting Jesus' ministry. In any organisation, the people working behind the scenes are equally as important as the people at the forefront. Jesus' ministry needed both sets of people. He had the twelve who were the public figures; they were at the forefront. But He also had the behind the scene foot soldiers who kept the ministry moving. Are you at the forefront or behind the scenes? You are equally important in God's agenda:

"Whatever you do, work at it with all your heart, as working for the Lord, not for human masters, since you know that you will receive an inheritance from the Lord as a reward. It is the Lord Christ you are serving."

Colossians 3:23-24

The Lord is counting on you.

Secondly, let's look at the calibre of people in this company. They were women who were grateful to the Lord for one thing or the other. Some had been healed from infirmities whilst others had been delivered from the chains of demonic oppression.

Gratitude makes service easier. It removes the burden of duty and puts on the robe of selflessness despite the cost.

The next time you feel like giving up in your service to God, or abandoning any good thing God has given you the capacity to do for His glory, think of something you are grateful to God for. You are needed in the assembly chain of God's work. What you do contributes to the kingdom of God, you are part of God's agenda.

Strategy

> Reflect on the goodness of God in your life and find ways of showing your gratitude through service. Find someone you can go out of your way to bless today as a result of your gratefulness to God.

Further reading

> Psalm 100

Day 5

Recover All

"With a blinding flash He destroys the stronghold and brings the fortified city to ruin."

Amos 5:9

Whenever I watch movies about Anglo Saxon times, I struggle to bear the bloodshed and the gory images of war. When a city is attacked, everything in it is killed and the remains of the city burnt to ashes. This was also the norm during the Old Testament times.

Israel defeated Jericho and devoted everything in it to the Lord. The booty of war carried away consisted of the weak and vulnerable who could not defend themselves: women, children and the poor. Often, the rejected and misfits who had no resources to rebuild what was left, were left alone.

In the scripture above God declares that *"With a blinding flash He destroys the stronghold ..."* The Lord is going to first of all strengthen every weakness. He will give you a new heart and a new mind. He will heal the sick and fix the broken. He will change the situation at the present.

The verse then goes on to state *"... and brings the fortified city to ruin."* So He will help you mobilise what you have and the new you to fight back and not only to stand in battle, but to overcome whatever had conquered you. He gives strength to the weak so that they can stand strong, fight back and recover their inheritance.

I don't know what looks like a stronghold before you. Is there something making you feel weak and inadequate?

God is able to give you strength and the grace to fight back and recover all. Imagine the weak and the feeble gathering momentum and now attacking the attackers! No matter how bad things may seem or how dead, Jesus says, *"I am willing ..."* (Luke 5:13) Receive strength right now in Jesus name.

Strategy

Pray and ask the Lord for boldness to act upon your faith.

Further reading

1 Samuel 30

Day 6

Do Not be Overcome by Evil

part 1

"Do not be overcome by evil, but overcome evil with good."

Romans 12:21

Everyone has an experience of pain in one way or the other which may have been caused by people we loved and or trusted. A betrayal or a rejection stabs deep into the heart. When a relationship goes wrong, so many other things come with it: tension, strife, bitterness and most deadly of all, unforgiveness. One may be tempted to react in order to redeem a scandalised image, to say something back or to give someone a taste of their own medicine.

But take a minute and reflect. Who has the say over your life and your pain? You are not responsible for yourself. Whatever emotions and resentment you may have harboured are against your Maker's will for you. You are actually not entitled to hold any grudge against anyone. Bitterness only stains us and hurt us. Hebrews 12:15 exhorts us, *"See to it that no one falls short of the grace of God and that no bitter root grows up to cause trouble and defile many."* Bitterness defiles us. Once you have no bitterness in you, you win!

When your heart is protected with the breastplate of righteousness, your next move is to overcome the source of the evil. Overcome evil with good! Be intentional about your thoughts - refuse to brood over the pain. Be intentional about your emotions: your spirit is in control of your emotions. Your spirit man is righteous and therefore your soul must align with who you are in your spirit. Put your spirit man in control, not your soul. The Bible states in Isaiah 53:5 that *"... the punishment that brought us peace was on him."*

Christ has already paid the price for your peace, therefore you are entitled to be at peace with God and man. Be intentional about your actions: begin to show love and grace to those who have hurt you. Let them go from the depths of your heart and as much as it lies in your power, don't treat them as they deserve. You'll begin to show mercy towards them because as the love of God overflows in your heart, you'll realise that they may actually need help.

Be not overcome by evil but overcome evil with good.

Strategy

Pray for the Lord to help you see those who persecute and abuse you through His eyes of mercy and grace. Pray for the grace to release them and to love them. Pray for the wisdom and maturity to handle things better in the future.

Further reading

Romans 12

Day 7

Do Not be Overcome by Evil

part 2

"Do not be overcome by evil, but overcome evil with good."

Romans 12:21

Lot lived in a land filled with so much evil, the inhabitants lived to gratify their selfish desires. The focus was on .me, myself and I'. The laws of hospitality were no longer upheld; for example, some visitors were in town and the locals wanted to have homosexual relations with them! The ancient landmarks had been moved so far away, everything was chaotic. Does that sound familiar?

Do you get bothered with the way things are going in your society? Are you concerned with morality in your locality? Are the boundaries being shifted in your office? Are the lines of decency being eroded from your relationships? Is truth being smothered from your home? The answer is - "do not be overcome by evil".

"Arise, shine, for your light has come, and the glory of the Lord rises upon you." (Isaiah 60:1). You are a carrier of the light of God. The opposite of darkness is light. Whenever there is darkness, a tiny ray of light will still be seen. Begin to do something about it, hold your ground. Don't be intimidated by the lies around you, just don't lower your standards. You can't change the whole world, but the world can change - one person at a time. Start with where you are - your family, your group of friends, your colleagues at work. When you stand firm in the truth, you will become the standard others respect. You may not be acknowledged

to your face but you will become the standard the people around you will look up to.

"Buy the truth and do not sell it." (Proverbs 23:23) The light in you is stronger than the darkness around you. The tiniest flame on a candle will extinguish gross darkness. You are the light of the world.

Go on and shine the light of God in you: one day at a time, one act of kindness at a time, one helping hand at a time, one gentle correction at a time. Extinguish the darkness of the world! Hallelujah!

Strategy

> Pray against sexual perversion in your community. Pray that God's purpose for marriage between one man and a one woman will stand. Pray that truth will be preserved in your family and society.

Further reading

> 1 Thessalonians 5

Day 8

Lay Aside the Weight

Therefore, since we are surrounded by such a great cloud of witnesses, let us throw off everything that hinders and the sin that so easily entangles. And let us run with perseverance the race marked out for us,

Hebrews 12:1

There is a weight and a sin that can easily entangle a believer. Every child of God needs to know that which easily entangles them. Note that this scripture talks about a sin and a weight. I won't go too much into explaining what a sin is because the Bible says our spirit bears witness with God's spirit that we are the sons of God so if we sin we know we have fallen short of God's standards.

A weight is any form of indulgence that slows you down. It is not necessarily a sin but it puts you first and God second. For example, over-pre-occupation with how your body looks, whether positively or negatively. There are some who look down on themselves and there are those who adore themselves so much it's just outrageous.

Also, appetite for food can be a weight, loyalty to friends who don't build you up can be a weight. A weight impedes your progress. Imagine running a marathon at the speed of a snail; you may finish the race eventually but it'll take you longer and you'll certainly loathe the experience.

Beloved, let us run with endurance the race that is set before us. Lay aside every weight so you can run the race that is set before you.

My race is different from your race but on that day when we stand before the judgement seat of God, we will give an account of everything we have done on earth and the things we should have done but did not do.

Lay aside every weight. Make things easier for yourself. Run your race without excuses.

Strategy

> Reflect on what needs changing or perhaps shifting in your life. Do your priorities need shuffling? Ask the Lord for the wisdom to keep your eye on the finish line.

Further reading

> Galatians 3

Day 9

Speak Life!

"He led me back and forth among them, and I saw a great many bones on the floor of the valley, bones that were very dry. He asked me, 'Son of man, can these bones live?' I said, 'Sovereign Lord, you alone know.'"

Ezekiel 37:2

The Lord presented Ezekiel with a situation - a valley of dry bones - and asked for his point of view. Everything looked dead and dry, yet God asked Ezekiel for his perspective. I believe in one way or the other God is asking us to give our opinion on our lives. God is mindful of our attitudes towards the things that are around and in us.

When faced with a situation, we need to speak the mind of God. Don't speak the challenge in front of you. God said to Ezekiel, *"son of man, can these bones live?"* In other words, son, daughter, what's going on? Do you think you'll survive? Will you pull through? God wants your perspective on the situation. Ezekiel threw the ball back into God's court and left it there. This I believe gave God the opportunity to demonstrate His power.

God's next move is dependent on you. If you call it dead, so will it be and if you call it alive, alive will it be! The power is in your mouth, on your tongue. With your words you decide your attitude and with your words you carve your way into your God-given purpose. Say what you want to see to yourself over and over again. Confess the Word of God to your spirit, soul and body. Command the Word over your life.

Begin to prophesy! Speak life to yourself. Prophesy unto every dead situation and see the breath of God quicken every dead thing. Speak life to that dream! Speak life to that idea! Speak life just like your Father God *"who gives life to the dead and calls into being things that were not."* (Romans 4:17)

Strategy

Cancel every negative word that has been spoken over you with the blood of Jesus and begin to speak the word of God over your life. Ask the Holy Spirit to quicken every dead virtue in you.

Further reading

Ezekiel 37

Day 10

It Takes more than Food

"Jesus answered by quoting Deuteronomy: 'It takes more than bread to stay alive. It takes a steady stream of words from God's mouth.'"

Matthew 4:4, TMB

At the end of the year, I was pondering over my health and the best way forward to maintain my fitness. As a wife, mother, church worker and career woman, I sometimes struggle to keep up a good fitness level. I just run out of energy.

So, I joined the gym, with the target of achieving two thirty-minute sessions a week. Ticked. The next target was a good dieting strategy to ensure I was eating a balanced diet. As far as I was concerned, I had done my best to keep myself alive and well but there was one thing that surpassed all my strategies - the Word of God.

Jesus said, *"it takes more than bread to stay alive"*. It takes more than a balanced diet and it certainly takes more than physical exercise. It takes more than the natural to stay alive. *"... but a steady stream of words from God's mouth"*!

Not just one word from God, but a steady stream of God's Word keeps us alive. Feed yourself with the Word of God consciously and unconsciously. Be deliberate about what you see and what you hear. The Word of God is spirit and life. Listen to good gospel music, listen to messages of sound preachers. Read your Bible every day and other sound Christian material. What do you feed your spirit?

Are you conscious of what is entering your spirit in your daily life?

Take a dose of the Word of God every day. Fill your soul and spirit with the Word, it is that which gives life and keeps you spiritually vibrant!

Strategy

> Ask God to help you by the power of the Holy Spirit to read and meditate on the scriptures daily. Ask the Holy Spirit to give you divine revelation into His word whenever you meditate on the Word.

Further reading

> Psalm 119: 65-112

Day 11
Be Alert!
part 1

"Once when Jacob was cooking some stew, Esau came in from the open country, famished. He said to Jacob, "Quick, let me have some of that red stew! I'm famished!"

Genesis 25:29

Esau did not place value on his birthright. He assumed that the favour he had with his father Isaac was either by chance or because of his hunting skill. Do not take the good things about yourself for granted because they are God given. James states, *"... every good and perfect gift is from above."*(James 1:17)

Secondly, he was overwhelmed by his momentary condition. He felt he was going to die of hunger. He made a careless negotiation as a result of his momentary condition. He did not consider his future. He was desperate. Esau couldn't see past his current circumstances. You have to live today with tomorrow in mind otherwise the devil will make you feel you have come to the end of the road. Esau's birthright was his God-given honour and destiny.

Do not be so overwhelmed by a negative situation that you sell your destiny. It is better to die in your destiny than live without a destiny. Mercifully, God is too faithful to let you go down. He will make a way, just hold on a little longer.

Don't be desperate. Don't be careless. Be careful who you speak to out of desperation. Be careful what you do out of desperation. Do not do something you will regret later.

Strategy

> Pray and ask the Holy Spirit to give you tenacity and resilience in the face of adversity. Pray that the perfect peace of God will keep you.

Further reading

> Genesis 25

Day 12

Be Alert!

part 2

> *"Jacob replied, 'First sell me your birthright.' 'Look, I am about to die,' Esau said. 'What good is the birthright to me?' But Jacob said, 'Swear to me first.' So he swore an oath to him, selling his birthright to Jacob. Then Jacob gave Esau some bread and some lentil stew. He ate and drank, and then got up and left. So Esau despised his birthright."*
>
> Genesis 25:31-34

Jacob tricked Esau but I believe it was not by chance. I believe Jacob had carefully considered how much their father loved Esau. There might have been something Jacob wanted, something he craved for that Esau had at his disposal. He might have even been jealous but whatever it was, it took Jacob on a journey of adventure and mischief to get his brother's birthright as the firstborn son.

Being a firstborn son meant a double portion of the father's inheritance and honour in the family. Jacob took the firstborn birthright from Esau without a fight, without a sword and without any confrontation. He took it with a smile and with a bowl of tasty food. Jacob's perfect opportunity came when Esau was desperate for food. He caught Esau unawares.

Peter admonishes us to *"Be alert and of sober mind. Your enemy the devil prowls around like a roaring lion looking for someone to devour."* (1 Peter 5:8)

The enemy is always looking for an opportunity. You can't afford to lose your guard. He will hit you hardest when you're down, therefore you cannot afford to be careless. Be vigilant, be aware of the people around you. No tricky situation is by chance, things don't just happen. You have something someone is after. You have something the devil is after. Be aware of who you are, what you have and where you are. Hold on to your faith, family, career, every good thing you have! Don't be careless.

Strategy

Ask the Holy Spirit to help you to be discerning when the enemy comes around you. Pray that henceforth, you will "know not any man after the flesh." (2 Corinthians 5:16)

Further reading

Genesis 36

Day 13

The Seed

part 1

> *"Listen! A farmer went out to sow his seed. As he was scattering the seed, some fell along the path, and the birds came and ate it up. Some fell on rocky places, where it did not have much soil. It sprang up quickly, because the soil was shallow. But when the sun came up, the plants were scorched, and they withered because they had no root.*
>
> Mark 4:3

The Seed is the Word of God and it needs space to grow in your heart. A seed goes through four stages: the sowing stage when it is planted, the germination stage when it cuts through the ground, the growing or maturing stage and the fruition stage when it bears fruit. First of all the seed has to be sown, and secondly it has to be sown on a good ground. What ground is your heart?

Often we get familiar with the Word of God. We think we know it all, perhaps after having heard it over and over again, and preached by different preachers in various ways. This attitude stops the Word from becoming effective in us, it stops the Word from making any transformation because we have very little or no expectation of what it can do in our lives. When our hearts don't have much soil, the seed of the Word will have no depth for it to grow. Our hearts are all shallow - *"... we can shout praise God , hallelujah"* - but our words are empty and fruitless.

The wayside ground is the heart that does not understand the Word of God; it hears the Word but can't process it or can't interpret the scripture. The devil comes along and quickly takes the word out of the heart. Understanding the Word comes by the power and fellowship of the Holy Spirit. A good Bible study group also helps us to understand the Scriptures.

Unless the Word is planted in our hearts, it does not have a chance of bearing fruit.

Strategy

> Does your heart have enough depth for the word of God to grow? Do you struggle to understand the word of God? Ask for the help of the Holy Spirit to show you the condition of your heart and to give you the grace to respond accordingly.

Further reading

> Mark 4

Day 14

The Seed

part 2

> *"He also said, 'This is what the kingdom of God is like. A man scatters seed on the ground. Night and day, whether he sleeps or gets up, the seed sprouts and grows, though he does not know how.'"*
>
> Mark 4:26

The Kingdom of God is like a farmer who sows seed in the ground. Day and night the seed sprouts and grows without his knowing. The Word of God is the seed.

Reading your Bible, listening to sermons, attending church and bible study meetings are all ways of depositing the seed into your spirit. Meditate on the Word, believe it in your heart, receive it into your spirit. Without your awareness, the Word will begin to bear fruit. A step at a time, a day at a time, little by little, the Word will bring a transformation in you.

Don't go too hard on yourself, get on with life as normal. With time every seed you have planted in you will grow and bring forth fruit. With time, your seed needs time. Every great structure needs a solid foundation, the deeper your roots, the higher your branches can grow.

To strike a balance, it's not just the Word of God that will grow when planted in you, bad seeds will also bring a negative effect if allowed to be planted into your heart. The judge of all things is time. Time will expose whatever you have kept in your heart. Keep sowing the seed of the Word. It will definitely grow!

Strategy

What distracts you from an effective Bible study? Ask the Lord to help you plan how to study your Bible.

Further reading

Proverbs 3

Day 15

The Seed

part 3

"All by itself the soil produces grain - first the stalk, then the head, then the full kernel in the head. As soon as the grain is ripe, he puts the sickle to it, because the harvest has come."

Mark 4:28

Maturity in Christ is not an overnight process. A seed does not become a tree overnight. It takes days, sometimes months or even years. In the same way our walk with Christ will not be an overnight growth. There's no such thing as a quick fix when it comes to things that need time.

Just as a seed first produces the blade, the ear then the corn, so we must mature gradually in our walk with Christ *"... till Christ is fully formed in us"*. The expression of Christ in us is different for every single Christian. Be patient and go through the growth process. Don't be in a hurry to reach for the sky when your root system is not proportionally deep.

One thing that's for sure is that for each season of growth, you get better prepared for the challenges ahead. I'm not insinuating a lazy 'leave it to God' attitude, but I want to encourage you to be mindful of your growth process. Use time to your advantage and prepare for every blessing and battle ahead. Growing is normally not very enjoyable but unless you can walk, God will not ask you to run. If you have not led a handful of people successfully, God will not give you a hundred to lead, let alone a thousand.

David had the boldness to confront Goliath because he had the victories of killing a lion and a bear under his belt. Experience comes with growth. Don't endure your growth, enjoy it and be ready for your time. Receive grace to abound in Jesus' name.

Strategy

In what areas of your life are you at a seed stage and what areas are you at a blade stage? Ask the Lord for the wisdom to be ready for your time.

Further reading

Ecclesiastes 3

Day 16

What are You Uprooting?

> *"See, today I appoint you over nations and kingdoms to uproot and tear down, to destroy and overthrow, to build and to plant."*
>
> Jeremiah 1:10

I live in a community that underwent redevelopment a couple of years ago. There was a steady influx of planning approvals and updates coming through my letter box. Then tractors and skips of all shapes and sizes arrived to begin the redevelopment. Dilapidated infrastructure was pulled down, broken into smaller pieces and transported away. Valleys and low-lying fields were all filled to prepare the ground for new schools, modern affordable housing and a doctor's surgery.

The old had to be pulled down to build the new. In the scripture above, God gives us a similar mandate: to overthrow, pull down, uproot and destroy. Thankfully, He also wants us to plant and to build. If you read the book of Jeremiah, you realise that he was living in a degenerate society and Jeremiah was the mouthpiece of God to fight against the norm and establish the will and intent of God.

In the same way, God is giving you and me the mandate to pull down, uproot, overthrow and destroy anything contrary to the Word of God around and in us. And in its place, plant the Kingdom of God and build it up. We have the mandate to plant and to build truth, the fear of the Lord, righteousness and love.

The authority is in your words. Root out kingdoms, pull down strongholds, destroy arguments and throw down any high thing that is exalted against the will of God. What are you pulling down with your words? What are you planting with your words? Don't be silent, begin to speak up, begin to decree things according to the Word of God and see them happen. Speak out in faith and exercise your divine mandate!

Strategy

> Release your faith and exercise spiritual authority over anything that is contrary to the original intent of God for your life.

Further reading

> Jeremiah 1

Day 17
Selah!

"Now the Israelites were in distress that day, because Saul had bound the people under an oath, saying, "Cursed be anyone who eats food before evening comes, before I have avenged myself on my enemies!" So none of the troops tasted food."

1 Samuel 14:24

In the chapter above, the Israelites were in a terrible battle with the Philistines. To describe how bad the situation was, the only Israelites who had swords or any sharp weapons were King Saul and his son Jonathan. It was a desperate situation but the Lord delivered the Philistines into the hand of the Israelites through Jonathan.

As the soldiers started advancing in the battle, King Saul, the Commander in chief, declared a fast until the battle was over!

Saul made a very poor decision; in fact, it was a life-threatening decision to declare a fast when the army of Israel needed food and drink to sustain strength for victory in the battle. It was poor judgement. Secondly, the Lord himself had planned an ambush of the Philistines on behalf of the Israelites. Saul had no basis whatsoever for taking credit in the upcoming victory of his people. Instead of being a part of what God was doing, Saul wanted to make himself relevant at all costs. He imposed a careless sanction on his army which could have resulted in them losing a battle that God had supernaturally given into their hands.

How and why do you make your decisions?

Not every situation demands your intervention. Learn to recognise when God is in charge and let God be God. Let others shine when it is their season. Saul had no business declaring a fast and a curse on soldiers who needed food for strength in a battle.

Your decisions today will go a long way to determine your future successes or failures. Before you make a rash decision, pause, think. Reflect. Selah!

Ask yourself these few questions: how does this decision affect me now? What will be the implications tomorrow and how will it affect the people around me? Don't put the people around you in jeopardy because of poor judgement. Don't be short-sighted. Don't be selfish. Your decisions today have lasting implications on you and the people around you. Pause, reflect and think about the long run. Take responsibility.

Strategy

> Pray and ask the Lord for grace to consider others before yourself. Ask the Lord to help you search your heart and remove any trace of selfishness and pride from you. Ask the Lord to help you to walk in the full assurance that you are no less or no more than who He says you are.

Further reading

> 1 Samuel 14

Day 18

Love has a Voice

> *"For God so loved the world that he gave his one and only Son, that whoever believes in him shall not perish but have eternal life."*
>
> John 3:16

There's so much going on when it comes to love. We talk about love, we sing about love, we pray about love, we condemn people who are not loving according to our 'standards'. We know that God loves us but it is time for us to just go ahead and LOVE. To love God and to love others.

The proof that we love God is in how we love others. Loving others is equivalent to loving yourself.

No matter how much you know, believe and embrace God's love, the love of God is not perfected in you until you begin to express it. I am not preaching good works, I am drawing your attention to the expression of Christ through you. God loved you so much that He gave his only son to die in your place. *"... for God so loved the world that He gave ..."* Surely after receiving this love and having been formed in the image of Christ, you ought to give back!

Give back kindness, give back love, extend a hand of grace to someone. Speak comfort to someone, value your neighbour, bring joy to someone. Put someone first, go out of your way for someone. Love gives *"... not looking to your own interests but each of you to the interests of the others."* (Philippians 2:4)

Your love for God speaks when you give everything to Him: your mind, worship, money, time, and heart. It is less of a struggle to share when we're grounded in the truth that we're stewards of all we have. But if we hoard and hold back, we'll be living in denial of God's love.

Love has a voice. Let your love speak.

Strategy

> What areas of your life are you withholding from God? It could be an area where the Lord has given you rest, where you no longer have to contend. Ask, with the help of the Holy Spirit to give back to Him whatever He has given you. Reach out to somebody today, not out of pity but out of love for God.

Further reading

> 2 Corinthians 8-9

Day 19

Cleave!

"That is why a man leaves his father and mother and is united to his wife, and they become one flesh."

Genesis 2:24

As early as the creation of man, God established the institution of marriage. Marriage is a union between a man and a woman. The scripture states, *"That is why a man leaves his father and mother and is united to his wife..."*

Before a man marries, he must be responsible for himself - not still eating from Mum's table or running to Dad at the slightest opportunity and for the least thing.

Cleaving is the process of becoming one as a couple - learning to know each other, tolerating each other, praying for each other and learning not to play 'God' by trying to change the other person. In marriage, two whole people cleave to become one whole being. This is very spiritual and a mystery, it fulfils the original intent of God when He created man.

He made the human being 'man' with both the male and female nature before separating man into distinct male and female genders. *"So God created mankind in his own image, in the image of God he created them; male and female he created them."* (Genesis 1:27)

A man and a woman must then cleave, become one before they can realise the original mandate of God. It is therefore very clear that your marriage determines, to a very large extent, your success in life. If you're married, cleave to your spouse. If you're yet to marry, take time to prayerfully choose your soulmate. God commands a blessing wherever there is unity. (Psalm 133)

Strategy

Invite the Lord to be the head of your marriage. He is the inventor so surely He's the best person to show you how to 'work it'. Pray for wisdom to be one with your husband or wife.

Further reading

Genesis 1-2

Day 20

Follow the Good Example

"Remember your leaders, who spoke the word of God to you. Consider the outcome of their way of life and imitate their faith."

Hebrews 13:7

Sometimes I'm alone and hard pressed. The work of the ministry is a "burden", a fire in my bones that can't be shaken off. I yearn for times of solitude to hear the voice of the Holy Spirit and to strengthen myself through scripture. A victorious Christian life is a day to day discipline which can be daunting, but the Word states, *"... remember your leaders, those who spoke the word of God to you."*

Consider servants of God who have gone ahead of you and emulate their way of life.

My discipleship teachers, Minister Kwame Owusu Ansah and Minister Charles Akrasi, inspired me. They deposited some 'fire' into my spirit that makes me want to go on when the going gets tough, they mentored me in the faith. Although they were not senior pastors, the love, humility and commitment with which they cared for the flock in their care was an example.

Reflect on their way of life - despite going through some tough times, God has not disappointed them. Some of the Christians who have impacted my world have had betrayals here and there, family tragedies, media slander, to name but a few. Our Lord Jesus himself went through persecution; He was called the prince of demons in

Matthew 12:24. Yet He stayed focused and kept his eye on the cross.

Are there any lessons to be learnt from their lives, what they've endured and what they've enjoyed? Consider the outcome of their way of life. Study their way of life, ponder over their life experiences and imitate their faith. Beloved, keep your eye on Christ, keep on keeping on, don't quit, don't be discouraged and don't give up. You cannot make it alone in the work of God, neither can you single-handedly do all the work of God. Have a mentor, someone you respect who has ploughed the way you are ploughing now. God has sent people before you. Consider their way of life and imitate their faith.

I am much wiser now. I read my Bible, pray, and listen to tapes of good Christian teachings so that, by the time I turn up to church, my faith is ablaze with the fire of the Holy Spirit!

Strategy

Reflect on the life of someone who has made a positive impact on you. Ask for the grace of God to abound on that person and a double portion on you.

Further reading

Hebrews 10

Day 21
A Man's Life ...

"Then He said to them, 'Watch out! Be on your guard against all kinds of greed; life does not consist in an abundance of possessions.'"

Luke 12:15

At different stages in my life I have taken pride in something about myself. For example, I have been determined to be a career woman in addition to everything else. The most sacred aspect of my life where I thought I'd put in my hard effort was my career until the Holy Spirit dropped the revelation into my spirit that *"life does not consist in an abundance of possessions."*

Your life does not consist of what you have so be careful not to fall into the habit of amassing possessions. Gaining more possessions can easily become your incentive. You get paid in a job so don't build your self worth around your job: your value is not your job title. Money should not be your primary incentive; honour and respect can also be an incentive; association can be an incentive – in other words, doing something in order to be welcomed into a certain group of people. If you support a cause because of the prestige you will gain, that will surely not be a reflection of who you truly are.

Who you honestly are is what you do without any incentive, applause - the thankless duties that may not be necessarily seen but which add value to humanity, or put a smile on someone's face ... that is who you are.

Brothers and Sisters, your profession is not who you are. If God took away your profession, education, social status or family, what would you be left with? So if you're a Pastor, who you truly are, is what you do outside your pastoral duties by going the extra mile to add value to some else's life.

A man's life does not consist of what he has, your life is what you go out of your way to do without reward or selfish motive or incentive. That is who you truly are.

Strategy

Ask the Holy Spirit to search your heart. Is there any good you have done for a public or secret reward? Ask for forgiveness for any area where you have fallen short. God looks at your heart. Pray, ask the Lord for grace and begin to restructure your priorities.

Further reading

Luke 12

Day 22

Not Every Invitation is of God

"So she wrote letters in Ahab's name, placed his seal on them, and sent them to the elders and nobles who lived in Naboth's city with him. In those letters she wrote: 'Proclaim a day of fasting and seat Naboth in a prominent place among the people. But seat two scoundrels opposite him and have them bring charges that he has cursed both God and the king. Then take him out and stone him to death.'"

1 Kings 21:8

In the scripture above, Naboth had declined the offer of king Ahab, a very spoilt king who could not handle the rejection of his business proposal. Naboth became public enemy number one because he said a simple "no", with no hard feelings. He was a God-fearing man but the people around him were not: they were sycophants and filled with wickedness.

Thessalonians teaches us to *"reject every kind of evil."* (Thessalonians 5:22) If anything looks a bit dodgy, it has an appearance of evil and the Bible advises us to stay away from it. Beloved this is the point where we sometimes fall short, so we must not assume everyone's heart is right.

Naboth was invited to a meeting and given the seat of the guest of honour. Whilst making I imagine, an acceptance speech, suddenly some men accuse him of blaspheming against God and the king: an offence punishable by death. And for some reason, not a single person in that meeting stuck up for him. The meeting, the fast and all the prayers being said were a set up against one man! It's amazing to what extent the enemy will go to make sure you fall. It was Naboth's word against hundreds of people. His friends, religious leaders and honourable men picked up stones and began to stone him to death.

Not every invitation must be honoured, no matter how honourable your intentions are. Be discerning and decline when you're not sure of the motives of the people around you. There's nothing wrong in saying "no" for the sake of self-preservation. Evil always aims to attack good and the aim of darkness is to overcome light. May God help you to discern those who are with you and against you.

Strategy

> Pray and ask for the wisdom to be as wise as a serpent and as harmless as dove. (Matthew 10:15)

Further reading

> 1 Kings 21

Day 23

Consecration

part 1

> *"Do not give dogs what is sacred; do not throw your pearls to pigs. If you do, they may trample them under their feet, and turn and tear you to pieces."*
>
> Matthew 7:6

This scripture reminds me of the life of Samson and about my own life too.

Samson was an anointed man of God, whose destiny had been foretold. There are only three people whose destinies were foretold before they were born in the Scriptures: Samson, John the Baptist and our Lord Jesus Christ. The life of Samson in the book of Judges 13-16 is a life of betrayal and emotional blackmail. The women he loved blackmailed him emotionally and eventually betrayed him. When we consider the calibre of women who were in Samson's life, they were clearly not Israelite women.

Samson revealed a secret to his wife - a woman he was supposed to trust but she betrayed him and went on to marry another man. The next woman he was with, succeeded in capturing him because again he revealed an even bigger secret to her. It cost Samson his eyes and subsequently his life.

Brothers and Sisters, don't cast your pearls before swine and don't give that which is Holy to dogs. It's not in the nature of pigs to appreciate pearls neither will dogs appreciate Holy things. They will first of all trample upon them, then turn to destroy you. When someone asks you the secret of your success, take a pause and ask yourself whether it is worth telling them (that is if you have one). Of what value is that information to them? Will they value it as much as you do? Will they be grateful as much as you are? If not, don't cast your pearls before swine.

There was a time when I was an open book, I couldn't discern between Jack and Jones. I answered every question and gave everyone access to my thoughts. I cast my pearls before swine and they trampled on my pearls and attacked me big time! I am now wiser, by the grace of God.

Samson lost his strength. The Bible says when Samson's hair was shaved, the Spirit of the Lord departed from him. He shared his secret with the wrong person. Today, this week, this month, this year, may the Lord grant you wisdom to share with the right people. Don't give what is valuable to someone who will not value it.

Strategy

> Do you need to operate at an even higher level of wisdom in your speech and actions? Ask the Lord to give you a wise heart.

Further reading

> Proverbs 14

Day 24

Consecration

part 2

> *"One day Samson went to Gaza, where he saw a prostitute. He went in to spend the night with her."*
>
> Judges 16:1

What on earth was this man of God doing with a harlot? As I pondered on this text, I began to ask myself whether I have been equally guilty of such carelessness, and whether there are instances where I belittled the grace of God and grieved the Holy Spirit. Beloved, I am not trying to make you sin-conscious but I would like you to examine yourself.

> *"But just as he who called you is holy, so be holy in all you do; for it is written: 'Be holy, because I am holy.'"*
>
> 1 Peter 1:15

Without holiness we cannot see God. It is also very clear that God is not unjust to demand from us what we cannot achieve. He knows we can attain Holiness by His grace, and so that is why He asks us to be Holy. Holiness is a matter of principle. It starts from your heart: newness of life in Christ (2 Corinthians 5:17), then affects your thoughts: renewing of your mind (Romans 12:2).

When purity overflows from your heart, it will show in your actions. If we struggle to be pure in certain domains in our lives, it's an indication that we might not have fully surrendered that domain to God.

> *"... it is God who works in you to will and to act in order to fulfil his good purpose."*
>
> Philippians 2:13

Beloved, check your actions and your motives. Desire what's right, be at the right place, say what is right, do the right thing and think right thoughts. Sin corrupts and will eventually destroy whoever yields to it. The Lord said to Cain:

> *"If you do what is right, will you not be accepted? but if you refuse to do what is right, sin is crouching at your door; it desires you, but you must master it."*
>
> Genesis 4:7, BSB

In the same way, sin desires everyone of us but we, as children of God, must master it. Make a choice today to say 'no'.

Strategy

Search your heart and ask the Holy Spirit to reveal any un-surrendered territories to you. Pray for forgiveness. Pray for the Holy Spirit to lead you and sustain you in a life of purity.

Further reading

1 Peter 1-2

Day 25
Sweetness after the Battle

"Some time later, when he went back to marry her, he turned aside to look at the lion's carcass, and in it he saw a swarm of bees and some honey. He scooped out the honey with his hands and ate as he went along. When he rejoined his parents, he gave them some, and they too ate it. But he did not tell them that he had taken the honey from the lion's carcass."

Judges 14:8

Beloved, there is a time in life for everyone when you have to deal with some things. Samson was on his way to take a woman's hand in marriage, it was a season of anticipation towards a good thing, but out of nowhere a young lion came up against him. Sometimes just before a breakthrough you can face serious setbacks from apparently nowhere.

He wrestled the lion, killed it and carried on as normal. The Bible says he told no one about it, he kept it to himself. It's good not to get distracted by the ups and downs of life. Keep your calm and keep your focus on the greatness ahead. Imagine the 'pity party' Samson's family would have thrown knowing a lion attacked their son on the way to his engagement. If they had been from the part of Africa where I come from, they would have blamed all the witches in the family. But he carried on and told no one about it because something worthier was ahead of him.

Then after a while when he was on his way, on the same road again to see his wife, he turned to see the carcass of the lion and behold there was a swarm of bees and honey in the carcass.

Beloved, life presents us with different experiences. On the same road that he was attacked by a lion, he found honey. In the same season of time, he went through adversity and comfort. Same season, same path, two polar opposite experiences.

I encourage you, just as Samson defeated the lion by the Spirit of God, you too can overcome every challenge or circumstance that 'roars' against you. And after you have overcome that situation, you will find honey, sweetness, satisfaction, promotion and increase. Then you can boldly say, *"Out of the eater, something to eat; out of the strong, something sweet."* (Judges 14:14)

There is sweetness after the battle.

Strategy

Is there any circumstance that you need to deal with quietly with the help of the Holy Spirit? Ask the Lord for all that you need. It is already provided.

Further reading

Isaiah 43

Day 26

The Old Prophets

> *"Now there was a certain old prophet living in Bethel, whose sons came and told him all that the man of God had done there that day. They also told their father what he had said to the king."*
>
> 1 Kings 13:11

A young prophet was sent by God to deliver a fierce message to the king of Israel. There were several prophets in the land, but God chose this young, nameless prophet to deliver this great message. Remember this was the time when the ten tribes had rebelled and broken away from Judah.

The young prophet prophesied, backing it with signs and wonders. The whole nation was shaken. News spread around, and the word went out. The old prophet whom the Lord had not spoken to, persuaded the young prophet to go to his house and eat although God had warned him not to do so. *"... for I was commanded by the word of the Lord: 'You must not eat bread or drink water or return by the way you came.'"* (v. 9)

In the middle of the meal, this old prophet who had told a lie, now began to prophesy death to the young prophet by the Spirit of the Lord!

The lesson here is that God speaks to us individually and we are responsible for our entire obedience to the voice of God. We cannot compromise in any way. It's commendable to respect and honour people but God alone is to be reverenced above all. Don't compromise your obedience for anything. The young prophet in our story knew categorically that he didn't have to eat or drink in Bethel but out of respect for the old prophet, he sat down to eat with him when God had said otherwise. I'm sure the old prophet knew what he was doing. How dare this young man come to correct what he the old prophet had not corrected? How embarrassing for God to bypass him and speak through someone else?

Can I also boldly say that someone may have carried the anointing yesterday and may be living in total separation from God today. The fact that some were anointed yesterday doesn't mean they are today. The fact that certain people gave you good advice yesterday, doesn't necessarily mean they'll give you good advice today. Test all spirits.

Strategy

> You may have this one 'go-to' person in times of counsel; ask yourself whether this "go-to" person is still operating in the wisdom and spirit of God? *"Fear of man will prove to be a snare, but whoever trusts in the Lord is kept safe."* (Proverbs 29:25). The fear of man will push you contrary to God's will for you. Determine to totally obey every instruction God has given you

Further reading

> 1 Kings 13

Day 27
And God Remembered...

"But God remembered Noah and all the wild animals and the livestock that were with him in the ark, and he sent a wind over the earth, and the waters receded."

Genesis 8:1

In Genesis chapter 7, we read of the wickedness of the human race. Man lived without God and the sons of God came and married the daughters of men. Everything was just contrary to God's original intent. The world was in a mess and God was disappointed in man. The Lord wiped out everything He had created with a great flood. But the Bible says the Lord remembered Noah. In the midst of the disappointment and the chaos, Noah and the ark were a spark of hope in a difficult situation - God's only hope.

Sometimes life does not go according to plan: things crop up, people change their minds, unexpected events happen, we get disappointed, we feel betrayed and used BUT always try to look for something good out of the situation. God remembered the only man who was righteous on earth. He had just one man and his family out of the thousands and made a new world out of him.

Begin to restructure your life based on the good things. God did not focus on the bad, otherwise Noah and his family would have been forgotten in the ark and they would have perished as well but God remembered, restored and made a new covenant with them. Beloved, it's amazing how much positivity and strength can come out of hope. Begin to focus on the good, stretch it out and you'll have enough to rebuild every area of brokenness.

Strategy

Just as God did not forget Noah, He will not forget you. Pray for friends or family who need God's visitation.

Further reading

Isaiah 54

Day 28
Faith

"... without faith it is impossible to please God, because anyone who comes to Him must believe that He exists and that He rewards those who earnestly seek Him."

Hebrews 11:6

Imagine someone saying, *"I breath in and out but I don't believe the wind is real because I don't see it."* You would laugh in his or her face, wouldn't you? The fact that anyone breathes in and out is proof that there is something called air and the movement of air is clear to every living thing it comes into contact with. When the wind blows, the trees shake, the leaves fall, even cars and buildings can be blown away. Yet no one has ever seen the wind.

Similarly, God is real and God is God. Whoever comes to God must believe that He exists. Whoever prays to God must believe without a shadow of doubt that He is a living, hearing, speaking and doing being. He hears, He sees, He speaks and He touches. The fact that you don't see Him, does not make Him non-existent nor irrelevant. The fact that you can't physically touch Him does not mean He is fictional. When He moves, every living thing moves. When He speaks, the universe responds.

Beloved, believe that God is, and He rewards those who diligently seek Him. The word that qualifies the verb seek is "diligently". If you seek God diligently, He will reward you. If you are not diligent in seeking Him, you'll be chasing the wind and get nothing in return. Faith is the belief that God is and because He is, He will answer your prayer, glorify Himself and honour His Word.

Have consistent faith in God, and don't let your faith fluctuate.

Strategy

> What are you struggling to believe God for? Stretch your faith. Stick to the Word of God and you'll have a thousand reasons to believe that God will do what He says He will do.

Further reading

> Hebrews 11

Day 29

Praise!

"Through the praise of children and infants you have established a stronghold against your enemies, to silence the foe and the avenger."

Psalms 8:2

We praise God for what He has done. When we praise, we magnify God, and so tell of His true nature. We tell of how awesome, magnificent and mighty He is. We are ordained to exalt God.

The effect of praise is to make the enemy afraid. As the Scripture above states, *"... praise establishes a stronghold against the enemy."* Secondly, praise *"silences the foe and the avenger."* When we praise God, we build defences against the enemy, and the enemy begins to retreat. Hallelujah!

How big is your praise? Have you taught your children to praise God? How often do you tell of the goodness of God over your life? Complaining will not get the job done. But when we praise, God begins to arise from His throne, with Jesus the Son and the Holy Spirit. He starts looking for where the sweet sound is coming from. He looks around and then oh, He locates this person saying, 'Lord I praise you, Lord I love you, hosanna in the highest, Lord you're the King of glory!' He'll stay with you, His presence dwells in his praise.

Remember that the walls of Jericho came down with a shout of praise. Amidst praise, God begins to do what only

He can do! Praise the Lord! From today, I challenge you to become a praising Christian.

Keep a diary of all the things God brings your way, all answered prayers whether big or small. You will notice the difference in your attitude and an even bigger ripple effect in your prayer life and relationship with God.

Strategy

>Praise the Lord with your words. Find adjectives that describe who God is to you. Go on and shower some love on this awesome King

Further reading

>Psalm 145

Day 30
The Attitude of Christ

> *"In your relationships with one another, have the same mindset as Christ Jesus: Who, being in very nature God, did not consider equality with God something to be used to His own advantage; rather, He made himself nothing by taking the very nature of a servant, being made in human likeness. And being found in appearance as a man, He humbled Himself by becoming obedient to death - even death on a cross!"*
>
> Philippians 2:5-8

After reading this scripture we realise that there was an attitude that Christ adopted when He came on earth - this was the mind of Christ. That's why the Bible admonishes us to *"have the same mindset as Christ Jesus"* - the mind of humility. Christ was still God in all His fullness but He humbled Himself and made himself of no reputation so He could save you and me. He did not use it as a bragging right.

We can go through life wanting to be served or we can look for opportunities to serve others. Whatever the circumstance, the choice is ours to make. The power is in our hands to choose right. I have seen a lot of Christians complain in the house of God. They complain about every single thing and criticise every decision but don't want to commit to be involved because they have chosen the attitude to be served. Choose the attitude to serve and to look for opportunities to serve others and God, and *"... have the same mindset as Christ Jesus."*

Let's cast our minds back to the Christmas story. When Jesus was born, He was not born in a hospital neither did He even have a home birth. He was born in a manger! No family member came to visit Him rather He was visited by strangers. His father Joseph did not have a noble profession. His father could have been a doctor, a lawyer, or a mayor - someone reputable in the community, but He came as a carpenter's son.

For thirty years Jesus had to put up with people like you and me despite being the Son of God. He had to cope with nagging parents and siblings.

He had to put up with a community filled with sin although He was sinless and hated sin. But Jesus submitted to His environment and to the purpose of His calling. I don't think I would have passed the test but Jesus did. He was God but He lived as man for 33 years. Even when He started His ministry, people did not accept Him as God but He still remained humble.

In humility before the Lord, we are lifted up.

Strategy

>Pray and ask the Lord to give you a heart of humility. Read and meditate on 1 Peter 5:5.

Further reading

>Isaiah 14

Day 31

The Spirit!

> *"Suddenly a sound like the blowing of a violent wind came from heaven and filled the whole house where they were sitting. They saw what seemed to be tongues of fire that separated and came to rest on each of them. All of them were filled with the Holy Spirit and began to speak in other tongues as the Spirit enabled them."*
>
> Acts 2:2-4

On the day of Pentecost, the disciples of Jesus were all together in one place. They were praying and waiting for the promise of the Father. They were together in one place with one purpose according to the will of God.

Does this sound familiar? In Genesis 11 the people of the earth were all together in one place, with one accord, wanting to do something good. But their intention was against the will of God and God had to step in. Two similar situations, two different outcomes. Beloved, God sees your heart and responds to you according to the attitude of your heart. The Lord used confusion of the tongue to scatter men in times past but in the fullness of time, He used the same tool to unite His people by the power of the Holy Spirit.

When the Holy Spirit is on you, all things are possible! The disciples were timid, inexperienced men but when the Holy Spirit came upon them - remember they had already been filled with the Holy Spirit (John 20:22) they began to speak with different tongues as a sign of God's power. Beloved, what is in your hand? What dreams and ambitions are in your heart? What did not work the last time will work this time around because of your submission to the direction of the Holy Spirit. God will work this time because you are now in His will for you. If you have cast off selfish ambition and self-will, you are broken and ready to do His will. At the tower of Babel, men wanted to make a name for themselves by building a tower. They had the wrong motives. But because your motives are now in line with the will of God, you can begin to take the bull by the horn. You are strengthened by the power of the Holy Spirit.

You are a sign and a wonder. People will see you, listen to you and be amazed. Your life will be a testimony, people will give glory to God because of you! Hallelujah!

The disciples began to draw people for Jesus and on the same day three thousand people were drawn into the household of God.

Begin to step out into your destiny by the power of the Holy Spirit and watch the lives around you get drawn to you like a magnet. You are an answer to a need, you soar above every weight, every challenge and every setback. Be who God says you are - *"more than a conqueror!"* (Romans 8:37)

Strategy

Write down a vision that you have postponed until now. You'll need the Holy Spirit to help you. Now take a leap of faith and begin to run with that vision the Lord has laid on your heart!

Further Study

1 Samuel 17

www.ingramcontent.com/pod-product-compliance
Lightning Source LLC
Chambersburg PA
CBHW071751040426
42446CB00012B/2521